ENDURING THE NIGHT

COURAGEOUS STORIES OF SURVIVAL BY FORMER GIRL SOLDIERS

PRAISE FOR ENDURING THE NIGHT

It is rare when a book captures both the heart and the mind, penetrating to the soul. *Enduring The Night* is one of those books. The stories of the young women in this book provide deep insight not only into the desperation of the horrendous oppression of young girls in Uganda but also speaks acutely to a world that needs to wake up and take action. This book is a must read for any follower of Christ who is yearning to know what the Father is doing in the world. But, be forewarned. The stories in this book go beyond providing information. The stories in this book will drive you to action.

Al Van Horne, Board of Directors, Iron Sharpens Iron

Working amid the darkness of broken lives would be nearly impossible were it not for the great truth that the Light can overcome even the deepest darkness. *Enduring the Night* captures this truth and offers a compelling message for those whose lives feel broken, for those who serve the broken, or for those who need to be inspired with stories of resilience and redemption.

Michael Saccocio, Executive Director, City Mission of Schenectady

Enduring the Night—absolutely heartbreaking, compelling, and hopeful ...

As I've traveled the world, I've witnessed the anguish of children growing up in confinement and brutality. But nothing compares with the stories of innocent young girls kidnapped, tortured, brutalized, and abused by men of violence. Because this continues to happen in our modern world, we should awaken out of complacency and satisfaction to seek justice for those who continue to be victimized; to walk with Jesus into the horror and the trauma, bringing help, hope and healing to the vulnerable "little ones" - for the kingdom of heaven belongs to them (Matthew 19:14).

Ron Nikkel, President Emeritus, Prison Fellowship International

For years, ChildVoice has been a true beacon of hope for the children of Uganda, and other war-ravaged places in Africa. Now there is a powerful and moving book to tell this story. *Enduring the Night* also bears powerful testimony to works of mercy, redemption, and healing. Authors Kristin Barlow and Natalie Committee-Fath have placed us all in their debt by telling this story—it's one we all ought to know.

Kevin Belmonte, Writer and historian, author of *William Wilberforce: A Hero for Humanity*

Grace, and other survivors of the dark atrocities of war in Uganda, give us a rare look that goes beneath the sterile headlines and news photos. They take us into their world as children and give voice to countless others who often feel, and in most cases are, forgotten. These young girls are true heroes, revealing the power of the human spirit. We see God's face in them, and when we have the courage to become involved, we reveal God's face to them as well.

Dr. Scott Larson, Founder and President of Straight Ahead Ministries

These stories will move you. These stories need to be heard. We should care whenever anyone is exploited, suffering or victimized—and we should celebrate whenever a broken life finds restoration. Read this book, and you will find all the reason you need to care for the broken, and join the work for their restoration.

John Stonestreet, President, the Chuck Colson Center for Christian Worldview

Through gripping first-person narratives and stunning images, *Enduring the Night* honors the experiences of girls who have survived some truly traumatic events. This books offers a prophetic message, sharing stories that involve deep brokenness and pain while also calling us to partake in the life beyond, full of redemption, dignity, and hope.

Peter Greer, President & CEO of HOPE International

TENTHPOWERPUBLISHING
www.tenthpowerpublishing.com

Design by Inkwell Creative

ISBN 978-1-938840-06-7

10 9 8 7 6 5 4 3 2 1

TABLE OF CONTENTS

To the courageous women of northern Uganda,

and all those who have endured the night.

FOREWORD   *by Joni Eareckson Tada*

I don't know anything about suffering.

I know that sounds odd coming from me, a quadriplegic who has lived in a wheelchair for 48 years, has survived stage III cancer, and who deals daily with chronic pain. True, I know what it means to live with affliction, but I'm a Westerner. And most North Americans and Europeans will *never* experience suffering to the degree that people face in Uganda or the Democratic Republic of the Congo.

I don't intend to make comparisons, for we all know that affliction hurts no matter who it touches. But in central Africa, I think it hurts a little harder.

It's why *Enduring the Night* is so important. The stories of these young African girls rescued from sex slavery and torture simply *must* be told. For no one should suffer alone, and no one should suffer for nothing. That's our heart's cry when we hurt. And thankfully, the book you hold in your hands shows how the Spirit-blessed touch of mercy ministry has imparted some measure of meaning to these young survivors caught in a web of meaningless affliction.

Is that enough? Is the warmth of a smile, the touch of a caring hand, and the effort to bring restoration and renewal *enough* for these girls?

Through the decades, I have learned that when you're hemorrhaging human strength, answers – even if they are good, right, and true – can sting like salt in a wound. When you're decimated and down for the count, the "16 good biblical reasons as to why all this is happening" can come across as cold and calloused.

Sometimes the best answer is the soothing balm of compassion, as well as the chance to know the Man of Sorrows who understands suffering more than *any* of us. For when they hang you on a cross like meat on a hook – and you triumph through it – you have something precious and eternal to give to *all* those who suffer.

So please, don't plow through this book too quickly. *Enduring the Night* is *that* important. Savor its stories sweetly, digest its lessons prayerfully and act on their counsel intentionally. For no matter what measure or degree of suffering we may be experiencing, we can *always* learn the best lessons from those who endure the darkest of nights.

JONI EARECKSON TADA

Joni and Friends International Disability Center
Founder and CEO

FOREWORD   *by Norbert Mao Esq.*

 The book *Enduring the Night*, by Kristin Barlow and Natalie Committee-Fath in partnership with ChildVoice, is a powerful testimony of love across oceans. The story of Grace and other girls defying suffering, hopelessness and even death is told with clarity, conviction and compassion. This powerful book is a tribute to hope in the face of great odds.

In a way, this story is also my story. Gulu is my home. In 2006, after a decade of service in the Uganda national parliament, I retired and went back to Gulu District, an area the size of Rwanda, to lead the local government.

After being elected, I declared a few simple, but by no means easy goals: peace (or at least silencing the guns), ending the suffering of our people in the squalid conditions of the internally displaced persons (IDP) camps, rebuilding local government structures and supporting income generating initiatives.

People like Grace flocked to my office. As I listened to them, my heart wept. They came to me not because they wanted handouts, but because they wanted a hand up. This book amplifies their story which is also the story of the long suffering people of northern Uganda.

Eventually the guns fell silent, but the war wasn't over. No problem can be solved unless it is faced. ChildVoice was on the ground, and like Nehemiah the prophet, Conrad Mandsager faced the problem of rebuilding the young lives of northern Uganda wrecked by war.

I heartily applaud the publication of this book. Read it. You will be moved.

NORBERT MAO ESQ.

Former Chairman of Gulu District Local Government
and current President of the Democratic Party of Uganda

PREFACE   *by Conrad Mandsager*

I was first called to northern Uganda when a good friend who was working in the region described the tragedy there as the worst humanitarian crisis affecting children that he'd seen. After hearing his description of the tragedy that was unfolding, I traveled to Uganda in 2006 to see what I could do to help.

Grace was the first girl I interviewed at the Layibi IDP camp. At that time, about 90% of the population was living in such camps, having been displaced by years of civil war and terrorized by the militant group known as the Lord's Resistance Army (LRA).

Grace looked incredibly wild. Her son Christopher was also there and he was getting into fights with the other children who were taunting him for being a child of a rebel. We interviewed several girls that day, and what struck me the most was that none of them could even speak about what had happened. When we asked questions about their feelings, they could only talk around it, but they wouldn't go there. They couldn't deal with it. All I could think was that children should be free to laugh and play without care, and yet these girls were silent.

It wasn't until several years later that I understood this problem not only to be an issue of trauma but also of stigmatization. It has such an effect that many former child soldiers refuse amnesty and attempt to bury their past, rather than open old wounds and start the rejection process again. It's true there are many layers to it, including the view by many tribes in East Africa that girls are no more than chattel and are therefore rejected if they are an embarrassment to the family or if they provide no economic value. I have seen so much despair in the formerly abducted girls who manage to survive in the bush—driven by the hope of reuniting with their families—only to find that their communities reject them. I believe that it is the cause of much of the suicide seen in this population. In Grace's case, this rejection fueled much of the anger she carried.

That day when I left Grace in the Layibi IDP camp, I already knew what "success" would look like if we were to help girls like her—though we couldn't do anything to restore their childhoods, maybe we could do something to restore their voices. This is how they would heal from their trauma, be empowered and have a brighter future. One year later we opened ChildVoice, a therapeutic community, welcoming Grace and our first class of war affected girls.

CONRAD MANDSAGER

ChildVoice Founder and CEO

9

INTRODUCTION

"If we mourned all of those who died, then we would die of sadness. Instead, we will laugh and share their stories. This is how we honor them. This is how we survive."

CHILDVOICE EMPLOYEE AND
CONFLICT SURVIVOR

It is difficult to imagine a nightmare worse than the reality that has been endured by the children and families of northern Uganda. During the decades-long war beginning in 1986, the Lord's Resistance Army (LRA) abducted more than 30,000 children from their homes. Those who were not severely maimed or killed were forced to be porters, soldiers, and sex slaves.

By 2005, IDP camps were swelling and the incidents of sexual assaults and disease were increasing. Organizations were working in the region to provide short-term relief solutions for returning abductees and displaced villagers, but it was clear that more help was needed.

ChildVoice was founded in 2006 to respond to this crisis and provide a sanctuary for adolescent girls for whom short-term interventions were not adequate, including former child soldiers and sex slaves, child mothers, orphans, and other highly vulnerable girls. Since 2007, ChildVoice's Lukome Center has provided a therapeutic community for girls to recover from the trauma of war and receive the educational and vocational training they need to rebuild their lives.

It was at the Lukome Center that we had the opportunity to meet incredible young women like Grace and those who have walked with them on their journey toward healing. A former child soldier, Grace was abducted at age ten and was forced to live a life filled with unimaginable brutality. Driven by the hope of reuniting with her family, Grace was instead rejected by her community for being a former rebel. Her story is one of tragedy and triumph. Despite her trauma, she is resourceful, courageous, and strong—she is a survivor.

This book is not meant to be a historical work; rather, it is a compilation of stories of struggle and survival as told to us by war-affected girls. We seek to honor their memories and give life to their stories because we know all too well that they are not alone.

While Grace's story is her own, the underlying themes of human trafficking, the use of child soldiers, and gender-based violence rests on the shoulders of humanity and represents some of the greatest challenges of our time.

While peace has returned to northern Uganda, today there are 35 conflict zones around the world where children are growing up under the shadow of war. In recent years, the nature of armed conflict has changed in ways that result in even more threats to children. For the girl child, the threat is even greater. Girls are particularly vulnerable to abuse, exploitation, prostitution, and forced labor.

Worldwide, children are increasingly being used as instruments of war. The Trafficking in Persons Report 2013, published by the U.S. Department of State, found a 30% increase in the number of countries recruiting and using child soldiers.

But there are other risks for children living in conflict zones. Changes in technology and shifts in war tactics have resulted in the use of aerial attacks (including the use of drones), putting children in the direct line of fire. Additionally, there has been a recent increase in the use of child suicide bombers and child victim bombers. Many terrorist groups are targeting children specifically through attacks on schools and education, as demonstrated by Boko Haram, a terrorist group that abducted 276 girls in Nigeria in April 2014.

This book provides a glimpse into a continuing journey toward healing for one girl in one community. As we face our own trials, they remind us that despite the darkness, there is light.

We are inspired by the faith and perseverance of these young women who have found hope in the midst of despair and the strength to *endure the night*.

Sojourners and co-authors,

Kristin & Natalie

THEY CAME FOR US

"Be strong and courageous. Do not be afraid or terrified because of them, for the LORD your God goes with you; he will never leave you nor forsake you."

DEUTERONOMY 31:6

Grace

The day was June 8, 1996. We were going to the fields from the camp to get millet from our small garden. It was ten o'clock in the morning. We thought that it was the best time, the safest time. We were always in hiding in the bush or in the camp between 5:00 p.m. and 9:00 a.m. because that's when the rebels liked to come. We went after nine, but this time it didn't help us.

> I was with my sister when they took me.
> I was ten years old.

For as long as I can remember, there had been war.

In the beginning life was good. Maybe that's what I remember because I was still young, but Momma and Daddy were both there and we had lost only one child. We all loved each other. There was usually enough food, we had clothes to wear, and all the children went to school. There were eight of us and I was the third girl. I was close with my brothers and sisters. We did everything together—cooking, cleaning, fetching water, and grazing the goats in the fields. When we got up early in the morning to weed the garden, we would talk, laugh, and sing together.

Those were my favorite times.

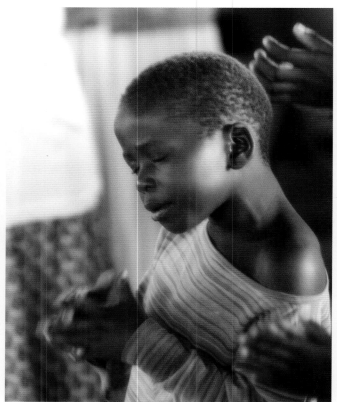

I sang in the choir at church too and I was so proud of it. Everyone knew that I was one of the best. I really wanted to go far in school, so I worked hard. Not everyone could do this, but I was competing with my brother Peter who was close to my age. We wanted to see who would do the best in school, and I wanted to finish first. I was very motivated and wasn't thinking about a husband or children like many girls my age.

Instead, I wanted to finish school and be a teacher one day.

As I grew older things began to happen in life that made me feel heavy.

My father took another wife and there were more children. Getting what we needed became more difficult. He was a hardworking farmer though, so we were still getting by. It seemed that the rebels and government soldiers were our biggest problem. There was always fighting. We fought the soldiers, we fought the rebels, and they all fought each other.

My family lived in the village far from town. We would work there during the day, but at night the children would go away and sleep in the bush to hide from the rebels. The earliest memory I have is one night when I was six years old. The rebels came to our home and broke my father's arm. It made me worry all the time. Before that, I mostly wanted to sit and play with the other children, but when Daddy's arm was broken, I didn't want to spend so much time with them anymore. I think I was jealous because their fathers were okay...they had two arms that worked well and weren't broken.

So I stopped being with my friends so much and stayed at home instead.

I remember thinking it was funny in the beginning that the rebels were only using stones and arrows for fighting, and I wondered why the army soldiers couldn't just shoot them all with their guns. Then they would be gone, and it would all be over! But they didn't. I don't know why. Later the rebels did have guns, and fighting them was even harder. They would come to our home, beat us and steal our food. The army soldiers did the same, threatening us and telling us we were rebels too. So I learned to be afraid anytime I saw a soldier.

It felt as if we lived in constant fear.

The rebels abducted many people in the community and even my older brother, Jacob. He was taken the first time in 1994. All the other children ran and hid in the bush, but Jacob was in a different house. He later escaped, but they kept coming back to get him.

This happened five different times and every time they came back, it was worse for us.

In 1995, I was abducted for the first time with Jacob and my sister Helen.

I was digging in the garden with my brother Peter and my parents when rebels came. They tried to cut my legs with the panga so I couldn't resist, but I kept jumping up to miss their swing. I remember my father yelling, pleading with me to listen to the rebels so they would not cut me. I fell to the ground and they started beating me with sugar canes. There was a lot of mud, so I forced my head deeper into the ground to avoid the major blows. After they beat me, they picked me up and I moved with them to Gulu town, carrying heavy loads for them for a week.

On the seventh day a helicopter came, and I saw my chance. I moved next to a boy who was hiding from the soldiers too. I remember our eyes met just before the rebels shot him. His body blew apart, pieces hitting me, his blood staining me. It was my first time to see this kind of death, but it wouldn't be my last. There were seven rebels and 40 children. I decided to take my chances and run, or I would end up like that boy. I ran all the way home that day. I ran from my captors into the safety of my family's arms.

But I soon found out that I would never again be free.

After that day I heard gunshots all the time.

I saw blood in the field. I found myself stepping over the dead bodies as if it were normal to live this way. At this time we stopped going to school; it wasn't safe. The rebels were smart. They would come early and ring the bell like school was in session. When children came, they took them.

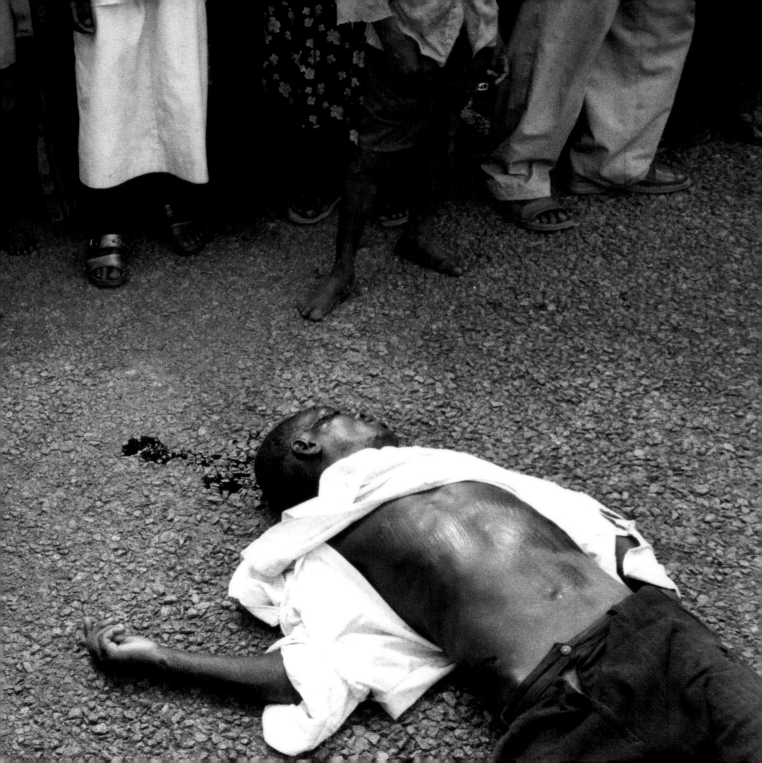

The day came when the army soldiers told us we could not stay at home anymore and took us to the IDP camp. I didn't understand. Daddy said I was still young. We had been moving back and forth from home to the camp for some time now, but today we left for good. To me it was not safer in the camp. I would still hear gunshots all the time, and the army soldiers would do bad things to us every day. But where could we go to be safe?

I heard life in the camps got harder and harder. But I don't really know because after one month in the camp, I was taken again.

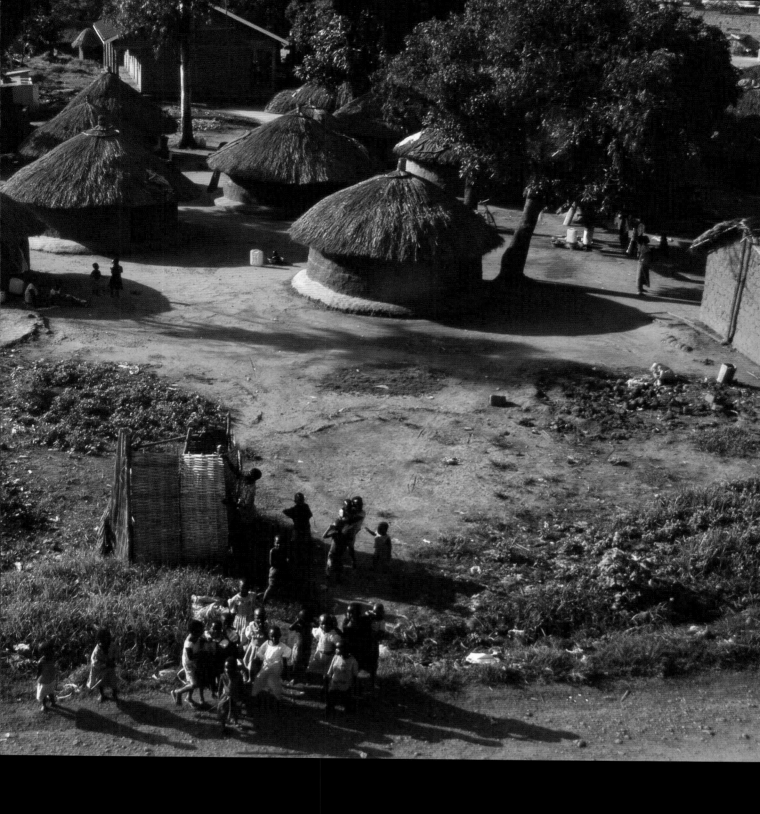

Beatrice

At a young age I decided I would be the only one to look after my life. My mother died when I was four and my father was not there. People said he lived in Kampala, but I never saw him. Instead, I stayed with my grandmother, but she could not care for me.

I slept in the bush so that the rebels would not come and take me in the night. I saw other children walking to town, so I started to do that. I would walk by myself to Holy Rosary Catholic Church because a lot of people went to sleep there. I walked four miles with my mat and blanket to get there. I defended myself, so no one disturbed me on those nights in town. Some of the children couldn't defend themselves; maybe they were too small or they didn't know. It was not good to get involved in other matters because it could cause you too much trouble. I saw this happen many times. So I kept to myself—just walking and sleeping. In the morning I would walk the four miles back home, go to school, and then walk back to town before dark.

I did that every single day for five years.

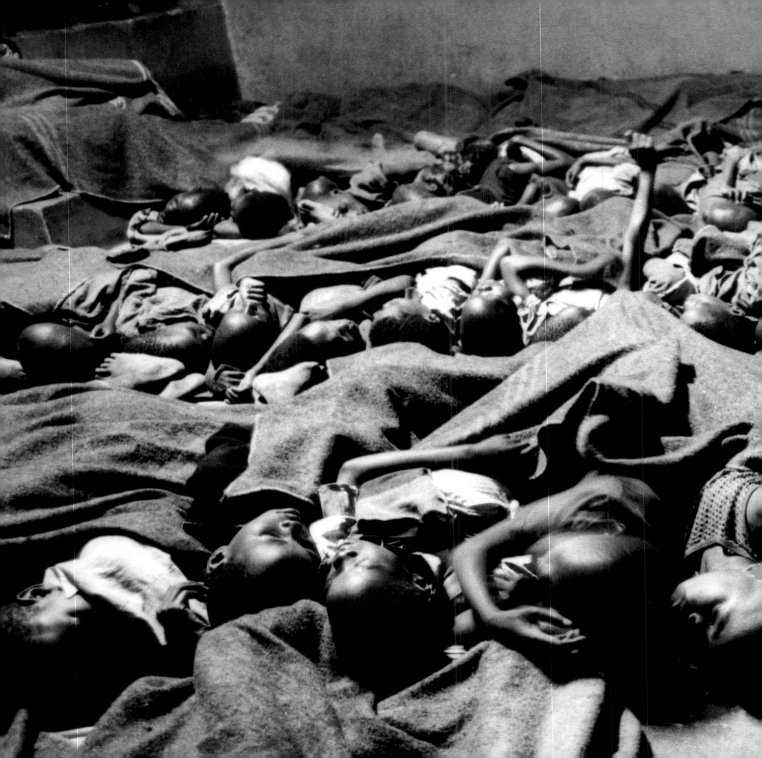

THE MARCH

"Therefore we do not lose heart. Though outwardly we are wasting away, yet inwardly we are being renewed day by day. So we fix our eyes not on what is seen, but on what is unseen, since what is seen is temporary, but what is unseen is eternal."

2 CORINTHIANS 4:16, 18

Grace

Momma was pregnant again, and the baby was coming soon. We were in the camp now and it was harder to get food since our gardens were far away, but she needed something strong.

She was getting weaker.

When the safe time came in the morning, my sister Helen and I left to get millet from the field. We walked a long time and hadn't taken breakfast yet. Before we reached the garden, we found groundnuts growing by the road. I told Helen we had to stop and eat because I was too hungry to move on. She was very nervous but she was also hungry, so we stopped, sat on the rocks, and ate. Helen finished quickly and said we had to keep going. I was still tired and told her we could rest just a little bit longer. When Helen didn't respond, I looked up at her. Her eyes looked past me.

I turned to match her gaze and saw their guns pointed at us.

I knew it was already too late to run.

There was nothing we could do. I recognized them right away as the same men who had taken me before. Fear paralyzed me, and I knew that if they recognized me they would kill me right away. Instead, they just grabbed us roughly, gave us large heavy bags of medicines to carry, and yelled at us to walk with them. The other children they had already taken were lined up and they looked frightened.

We walked some miles before stopping. All of a sudden I realized they were telling Helen to leave. They wanted her to run home and tell my parents that they had taken me, but I didn't understand why. She tried to look at me, but they threatened her and made her run. We did not even get to say goodbye. As I watched her run away all I could think about was Momma and how she would not get the millet she needed. I prayed she would still be okay. At least Helen was going home to take care of her. I could focus on that.

Then someone hit me from behind and told me to walk. I did. I looked at the others around me for the first time. We were all children, but we looked like goats, tied together in a line with rope around our necks.

We walked and with each step
I felt more and more alone.

I thought for sure they were leading us to our deaths.

It reminded me of the first time I met the rebels and they gave me a serious beating. I thought they would take me then, but they didn't. I don't know why they had spared me before only to take me now. What made them decide to let my sister go this time? I couldn't make sense of anything. I only knew they liked to kill people and I was afraid. I did not know then, but years later they would take my sister too. No one was spared in the end.

Steps soon turned into days, and I learned we were walking to Sudan. It was not easy. We had to carry very heavy things and I was small. It seemed there was never any rest. One time we were moving quickly and they made me grab a boiling hot pot from the fire and carry it on my head. In the bush, you do many things you didn't think you could do. We had to keep moving all the time. After many miles, many days, and many beatings, I learned to keep pace.

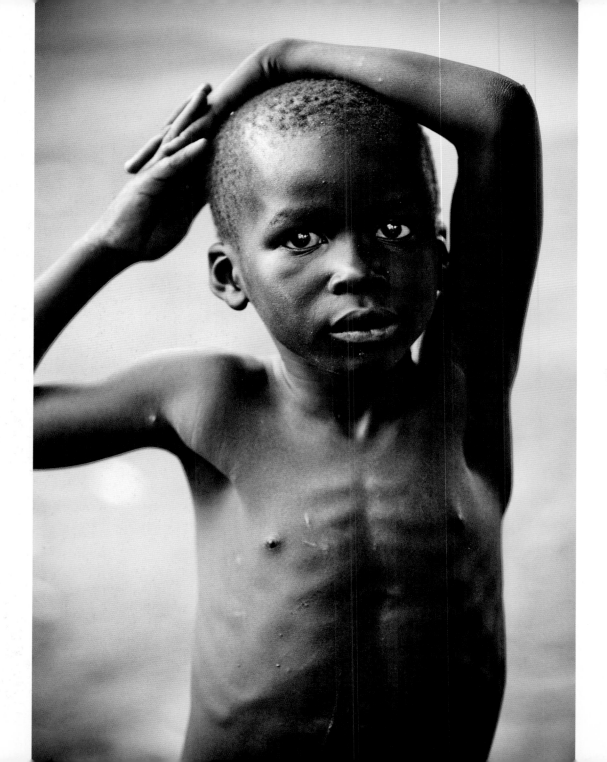

The hunger was also very difficult. In the beginning we mostly just had raw food and leaves to eat or whatever we could find along the path. Some children ate dirt. I was soon also eating many things I was not used to eating. I didn't think I would ever eat again like I used to at home. But the thirst was one of the worst things. I feared moving through the rivers because they were so dangerous, but at least I could sip the water, which was better than drinking mud. However, almost every time we moved in the water, the airplanes would find us. Their guns were loud as they flew overhead and they shot at us. Couldn't they see that we weren't fighting them? Couldn't they see our necks were tied and that we weren't there by choice?

Maybe they didn't want to see.

When the rebels first took us, they told us we would only be gone for a short time. I tried to believe them and not be so worried. But I also had to think of how to survive, and I knew that sometimes people could get away. From very early on in the journey, I thought that maybe I could escape like I had done before.

This is what I kept telling myself.
I would not wait for them to let me go.

But then I saw something that changed my mind. Right in front of me, they slaughtered a girl they caught trying to escape. I cannot even say now what they did to her, but I decided that day that I had to give up my dreams of escaping. I could only wait for them to let me go or kill me.

After six months, I was sure I would die in the bush. The rebels didn't even lie to us anymore because they knew we were too far away from home. Instead, they started saying I would never leave. Even if I escaped, they told me, all the people I knew at home would kill me anyway. I wondered if they were right. I had heard stories of people who made it back to their villages only to find that everyone there hated them and forced them out.

But my family would not do this—or would they?

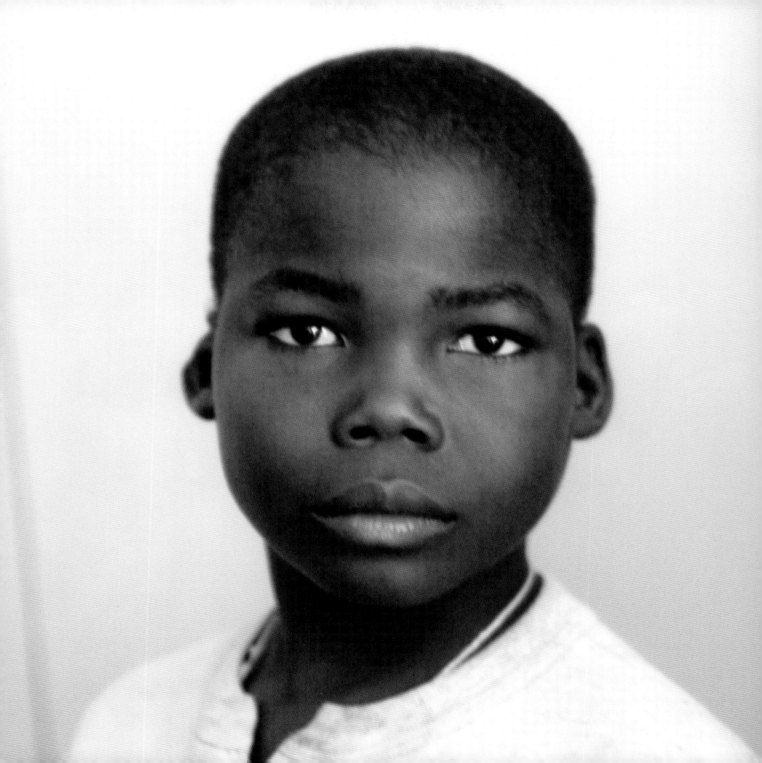

It seemed these thoughts were in my mind every moment, so much so that even when they gave us time to sleep, I could not. Instead, I would pray and whisper songs to God in my head. I asked Him for confidence, to make me strong, and to help me to survive. This could comfort me in the night. Even in the daytime my prayers continued, especially when we found ourselves being shot at by the soldiers. I could kneel down and pray right there and then. What else could I do?

I knew only God could protect me now.

Cecila

TEACHER AT CHILDVOICE LUKOME CENTER

*"I know that life is difficult for those who are captured, but sometimes
I wonder if the torture is not more for those who were left behind. I
remember everything, and there is no rest for me in all the days of my life."*

When the rebels captured my husband, I was away getting nails so we could fix the roof. When I returned home, he wasn't there. It was late, coming to 7:30. Finally, his brother came to our place and I asked why he was alone. He tried to deceive me at first, but I pushed him.

He simply said, "Where are Mom and Dad?"

His parents were at a funeral service and hadn't returned yet. He made a fire and said nothing. When my mother-in-law returned, my brother-in-law finally started telling the story.

These days, if you refuse to go to the bush with the soldiers, they will kill you right there. If you go, you will be okay for a while," he said. "It is better for you to be alive than to lose your life, so he went."

That was all I knew. I waited and hoped that I would see him walking through the field one day. This was the eighth time that the rebels had threatened my husband. He was an evangelist and would pray with people in the village center. The solders didn't like that, so they would cut him and beat him. I begged him not to go anymore, but he said that he must.

He said, "Dear, you shouldn't worry. I fear only He that can take my spirit, not he who can take my flesh."

But it did not take long for me to learn the true story of that day. This time, the rebels did not have mercy. They took him, along with the primary school teachers. They killed all of the teachers, removed their clothes and showed them to my husband. Then they gutted them. When they were finished, it was only the bones that remained.

They forced him to move through Kitgum District. When they made it to Palaa National Park, they met government soldiers and fought until they made a refuge there. That was the day the rebels killed him. I know all of this because one day my husband's cousin came to my home and told me. He had been a messenger for the rebels. Times were so difficult. Even those you loved could be forced to do bad things. He also brought a note from my husband who must have guessed his fate before it came to pass. He wrote:

> My Dear, don't you worry about me. What they wanted to do to me today, they have done. My body will go back to ash. I need you to care for my children well. Amen.

He wrote it and then he died.

I was only twenty-two years old. My children were four months in the womb—triplets.

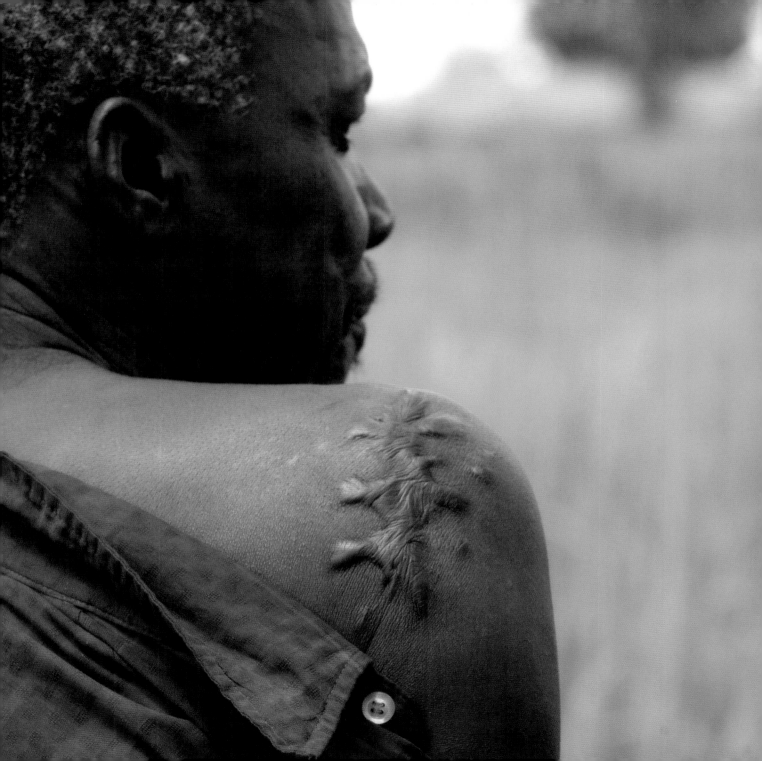

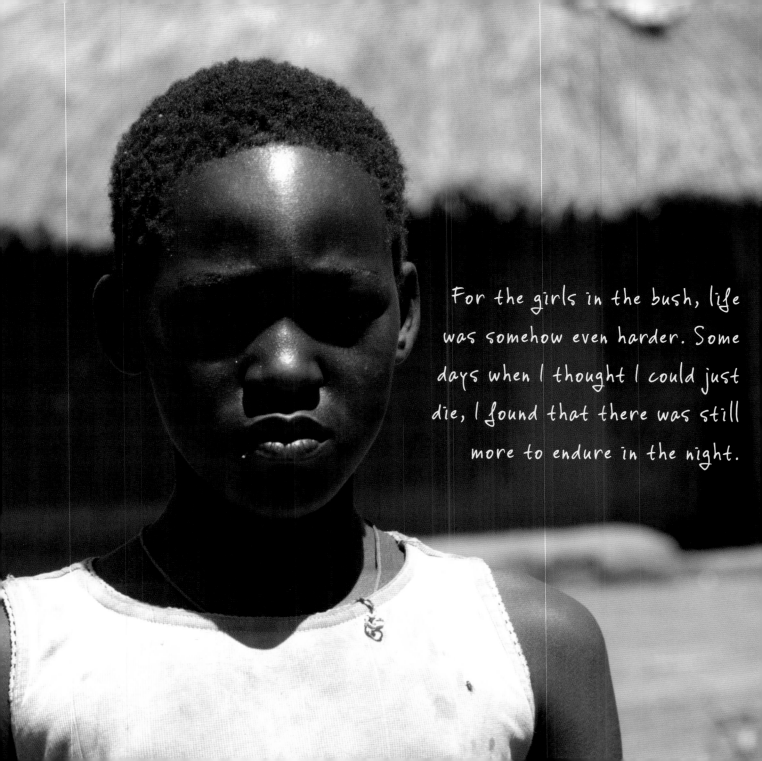

For the girls in the bush, life was somehow even harder. Some days when I thought I could just die, I found that there was still more to endure in the night.

HE TOOK ME AS HIS WIFE

Blessed are the poor in spirit, for theirs is the kingdom of heaven. Blessed are those who mourn, for they will be comforted. Blessed are the meek, for they will inherit the earth. Blessed are those who hunger and thirst for righteousness, for they will be filled.

MATTHEW 5:3-6

Grace

I was still young when they took me. An old commander they called "Lapwony" or "Teacher" took me right away as his wife, but he didn't touch me. He was kind to me and called me "Titinga" or "this one is still young." That is a name given to praise someone. He would take me for walks and we would talk. I almost felt like I had a father again. I began to trust him and believed that he would protect me. But the peace did not last long.

One night I was going to the bathroom when he came to me and forced himself on me. There was nothing for me to do about it. It was my first time. I was not yet twelve and he was forty.

Afterwards, I was physically sick. He forced me to follow him everywhere after that because he was convinced that I was going to try to escape. No matter what he was doing, I had to be there with him. He would take another wife or go to the bathroom, but it did not matter. He was always watching me, and I could not refuse him because he had a gun and could kill me.

Lapwony had 10 other wives, but he always wanted me every night. I knew that I could die if I refused him, but one night I could no longer stand it. I fought him. He was tired, so instead he went to another wife, but she refused him too. This was very bad then. I never forgot the punishment he gave us that night. He ordered us both to his room and said, "You both think you are the giants of the day, so let's see how strong you are. Don't move, don't shake, don't bend, just remain standing." He stayed half asleep in his bed and forced us to stand all night. We pleaded with him to let us go, but he refused. My body started to ache and swell.

The torture of not being able to sleep when you need it so badly is a horrible thing.

After two years as my husband, Lapwony died in 1998. Some say that he was thinking of defecting to the Ugandan army, so the rebel commanders killed him. I thought maybe that the commanders would have mercy on me because I had lost my husband. Instead, they gave me away immediately to another man called Tabulee.

Tabulee was also a commander and he had 25 wives. He was just as bad as Lapwony, always demanding sex. People guessed that he was thirty-two years old. I say "guessed" because most people did not really know for sure. In these times of war, it was easy to lose track of the days and months and years. I was Tabulee's wife for something like four years.

During that time, the rebels decided to make me a Brigade Commander. They taught me how to use a gun, and I became an active combatant in raids on villages. I raided villages mostly in Sudan but also some in Uganda. We would go in and take food, weapons and other things from people—whatever we could find that could help us to survive. One time when we were going into a village, I thought back to how rebels did this to my family. But I could never think about it again because now things had changed.

I thought being a Brigade Commander would at least gain me some respect. But I still had struggles because Lapwony's wives began spreading rumors that I killed him. Of course this could not be true, but I cannot blame people for thinking it.

A lot of bad things happened in the bush at that time. Things that sound strange, things that you cannot imagine a person could do...in the bush, they are real.

Ever since I was very small, I prayed and believed in God. I am sad to admit it now, but there were dark times like this in the bush when I doubted. I saw so many bad things and suffered so much that I began to think that God could not be here.

I felt so alone. I started to believe that I really was.

At this time, I was really at my lowest. I continued to carry a lot of heavy loads and was always so tired. In earlier days, I could find strength and continue, but now I was really so low. I soon found out that I was pregnant. I thought I was only sick for a long time because I didn't know how you should feel when you're pregnant since we did not have doctors in the bush. I could not rejoice, but I could not be sad either.

When I came back from camp fighting and raiding, I found that Tabulee, the father to my child, had been killed. He was shot dead while fighting in Soroti.

I did not expect it, but some part of me felt very empty that day.

I shut myself off from everyone and didn't have any friends.

I was still scared and angry, but as time went on I began to learn the way of things in the bush. I knew I could not continue to be alone. I had to start making friends.

So I tried helping the other children as they arrived. I would give them advice on how to live there. I would say things like, "If this soldier is angry, you must be very careful," or "If they say this, be careful, they are just trying to trick you." I started to make friends with these children because I was helping them. In return I gained courage because they trusted me, and eventually they even helped me too. Sometimes we could sit together and talk about normal things, about our lives before the bush.

I even started to laugh again.

Prossy

I was raped for the first time when I was ten years old. I was given as a wife to a Brigade Commander. The first time he forced me, it hurt so much. I bled a lot and I cried, but he had a gun next to him and I had seen him use it, so I had to stop crying. Every day he called me like this, and every day I would have to go. If I fought him, he would beat me so badly that I could not move. Then sometimes I would be so weak because there was no food or water, but still I had to go to him. There were 20 wives in all. If a rebel raided a village and abducted a beautiful girl, she would be his too.

Since I was also a soldier, I was more respected than some of the other girls. When the Brigade Commander would go away, I had to stay with the other wives and threaten them badly if they tried escape. The truth is, I would have been killed otherwise.

When he went away to fight, it was also worse because other men could have me anytime, anywhere they wanted. They called this "firing squad." If you refused, you were killed. On other days when the army would attack and everyone would run in many directions, other rebels would grab me and rape me right there in the bush. They did it violently, painfully, without caring at all. I eventually stopped fighting them.

It was as if something in me had died, and I no longer knew who I was. I decided that whoever I was, I could not be me.

BRUSH WITH DEATH

*"The Lord is with me; I will not be afraid.
What can man do to me?"*

PSALM 118:6

Grace

One day after we looted from a village, the rebels gave me a bag of food to carry, but it was too heavy and my chest started to swell. As I tried to walk, a boy I knew from my home came next to me and took the heavy load from my head. He gave me his gun to carry instead and we continued walking. Another woman saw what happened and she became jealous. So she went to the commanders and told them that we were having inappropriate relations.

The rebels approached us about this matter and we denied the woman's words, but there was no room for explanation. Instead, the commanders blindfolded us and brought us before the leader, Joseph Kony. When he heard the story, he said the truth will always come out—if we are innocent we will live, but if we are guilty, then we cannot live.

It seemed the rebels were ready to kill us either way because that is what they were trained to do, even without reason. The commanders took us away and told us to prepare because we would die that day at two o'clock. They gathered guns and rope and then blindfolded us as they tied us to a tree. They were making plans quietly, but we didn't know what they were going to do. I started praying that they would just kill us right then and not delay.

If death was here, I just wanted to die and not wait for my death in torture.

When two o'clock came, they brought a crowd of others around to watch. We were going to be an example as if to say, "This is what happens when you disobey." I could not see anything, but I heard the commanders laughing and making jokes as they got ready. Of course, I had seen this done many times already to other people.

We heard their rifles click into place and I took a large breath. I exhaled slowly...at least it would be quick.

But the shots did not come. Instead, I felt someone removing the blindfold from my eyes. Then one of the commanders spoke in a low tone saying that Kony had decided we should not be killed. Many of the men were angry and they beat us very badly that day, but we survived. After that, we were separated and I never saw the boy again. When people ask me if I believe in God, I tell them this story. I have seen the rebels kill so many people and for much less. Why not me?

After that day, I began to pray again and I never stopped.

Sabina

The rebels have taken many things away from me. In 2003 they killed my son, Isaac. He was sixteen years old and he was meant to start secondary school. The next year they attacked our village and captured me. They raped me many times and made me carry heavy things. I carried two basins of beans, one 10-liter jerrycan of oil, and a goat. One day while we were walking, a plane flew by overhead and there was great confusion. The chaos caused me to spill some of the beans and release the goat by mistake. The rebels got so angry that they beat me with sticks and a panga. Then they cut my stomach open with a knife. After doing all of that, they made me walk about a mile with them.

I dragged my body along somehow.

When they were distracted, I threw myself between a big tree and an ant hill. When they turned around, they couldn't see me. They looked around and even came very close to where I hid. I just closed my eyes, wishing to be invisible. They slashed at the grass with their bloody pangas, and I heard them say that they should have killed me when they had the chance. When I couldn't hear them anymore, I just collapsed and fell asleep, wondering if I would ever wake up again.

The next day when I awoke, I felt so much pain that I could barely move. A woman from Lukodi found me there. She had also escaped and she helped me get back to the village. When I got there my neighbors took me to the hospital where I stayed for two weeks. They treated my wounds and gave me medicine. They also tested me for HIV.

Thank God, I was negative.

My body was starting to heal, but some of the wounds were so deep that I knew I would never be able to farm well again.

Not long after I returned, the government soldiers forced us to move to the IDP camps. I stayed in the Coope IDP camp for two years and in the Lukodi IDP camp for another two years. Life became so difficult there. I had no money and no way to get money. I did not know how I would feed the children each day. There was never enough. I was overthinking all the time. I would even see dead people sometimes—especially my son, Isaac. I found myself even talking to him sometimes as if maybe this could all be a bad dream. I had no hope for my life or for my children or grandchildren's lives.

I just wanted to pass from this earth.

THE WAY HOME

The Lord is my light and my salvation; whom should I fear?
The Lord is my life's refuge; of whom should I be afraid?
When evildoers come at me to devour my flesh, these my
enemies and foes themselves stumble and fall. Though
an army encamp against me, my heart does not fear;
Though war be waged against me, even then do I trust.

– PSALM 27:1-3

Grace

I spotted Daddy coming home from the garden with fresh millet. Momma,

Helen, and I were just finishing dinner. We took turns washing our hands and

sat down together to eat. The maize posho stuck to my ribs and warmed

my belly. Later, we would sit around the fire and Daddy would tell us stories.

I smiled and my heart was full.

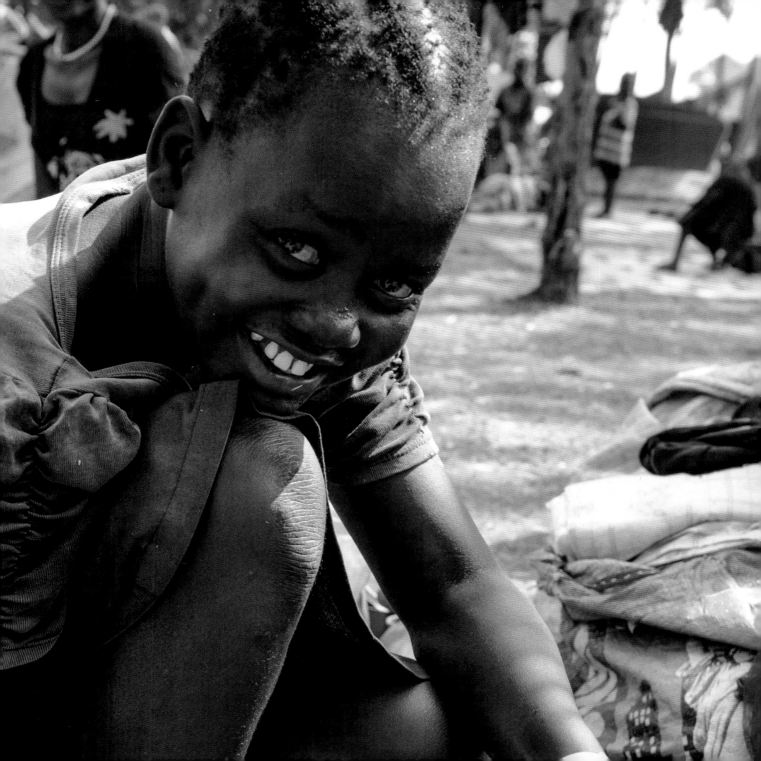

I awoke abruptly from my dream to a jab in my side and the sound of people arguing. We had to move now because someone had seen a government soldier. We would fight today. Bittersweet thoughts of my dream still lingered, and I quietly prayed for my family, begging God to keep them safe. Fear of the unknown was eating away at me—bringing me physical pain. What if they had been badly beaten or killed? What had happened to Momma and the baby? How was Daddy and his crippled arm? Who was helping with the goats in the garden? And who was bringing Daddy his evening tea? Maybe these dreams from God kept me alive, giving me small reasons to hope. Whatever it was, I knew I had to get home somehow; otherwise I would die, perhaps by a wound, but most certainly by sadness.

The gunshots brought me back to my senses—the soldiers had found us. I felt a sharp jolt to my back and fell face forward to the ground. What was it that forced me down? For a moment I thought I had been shot, but I quickly realized I was not bleeding. I looked up from the ground and saw chaos all around me.

Then it was clear—this was my chance to escape.

Everything went silent as thoughts raced through my head. *What if I got caught? How would I find my way home? How would I survive?* And it wasn't just me anymore. *What about the small child growing inside of me? Did I care what happened to that innocent life?* Emotions left over from my dream became so strong and took over my body. I felt myself begin to crawl in the direction of the trees. I kept going, afraid I'd be killed for sure if I stopped. My body kept going, moving against the ground until it could do so no longer. If the rebels caught me, they would kill me for trying to escape. If the soldiers caught me, they would also kill me because I was a rebel.

When I finally stopped, I realized that I did not know where I was. I needed help, but who I could trust? Then I remembered some of the children talking about a man somewhere close by who was working with the rebels. It was dangerous, but he was my best chance.

I moved through the night until I found his home.

My heartbeat was so loud as I walked up to his door. What if he gave me back to the rebels or told people in the village about me? They would kill me for sure. He opened the door, but he did not seem surprised to see me. He welcomed me in, gave me food and told me where I would sleep. I told him that he must take me to the place where they take the returnees. He smiled, but told me we must wait until morning.

That night I could not sleep—and then I heard them, people in village yelling, "Where is she, where is she? Where is the rebel?" I didn't even think. I ran out of the hut and into the bush outside.

Crouching down and keeping vigilant, I did not close my eyes once that night.

It was dangerous for the man to help me, but for some reason he did. Maybe he sensed my desperation or noticed my stomach that was beginning to grow. I don't know. In the morning, he got us bicycles and said he would lead the way to the reception center. While we were riding, I was very careful the whole way. I followed him at a distance, still fearing he would lead me to the rebels.

When I saw the center for returnees, my heart relaxed.

At the center, there was a mzungu [white person] who looked like a priest. I told him that I wanted to go home. He said he would take me to Gulu town—a place where they could help me more. We went by car and I stayed very quiet the whole time. He tried a few times to get me to talk, but I could not answer. When we arrived in Gulu, I finally spoke and told him again that I needed to go home.

I needed to find my family.

We kept driving in silence until I suddenly saw a boy I knew from my home village. I jumped out of the vehicle and ran to him. I fell on him immediately and cried for the first time since I had escaped. It was as if seeing him made it all real. At first he was alarmed, but when he saw my eyes he also started to cry. We were there in the middle of the road, just crying together. We didn't say a word to each other. We cried for all that we had known and all that we had lost. I wanted the boy to take me home, but the mzungu insisted I stay with him instead. He would not leave me, and he told the boy to tell my parents where they could find me. I watched out of the back window of the vehicle as the boy stood with his bike in the middle of the road. I wondered if I would see him again.

After all that, I could not even remember his name.

We finally arrived at a mission house. This was another safe place where they would take returnees, but I didn't know that then. The mzungu priest gave me food right away. I was desperately hungry but even more afraid to eat. The rebels told us we should never eat their food. So I watched carefully as he ate first. We shared from the same bowls, so I ate the same piece of food that he ate.

I followed his every move.

Who was this white man who spoke like an Acholi [a member of her tribe]? I couldn't trust anyone. After dinner, he showed me to my room. I told him I would not stay or sleep unless I could lock him in his room first. I was afraid he would kill me in the night. He had been nice to me so far, but I couldn't help but be afraid. He looked at me for a long time when I said that, but he didn't speak. He seemed to be searching for something to say. Somehow, he agreed to let me lock him in his room.

I fell asleep feeling a little safer this way, and the next morning I let him out.

The next day I told the mzungu again, "I must go home. I have to see my parents and my family." He said my parents were on their way to the mission house, but it wasn't safe for me to leave yet. I just had to wait a little bit longer. I didn't really understand. Now I thought they wanted to hold me like a prisoner, and I became even more nervous. (Later on I understood that this is how they cared for all the returnees to help them and keep them safe.) I tried to keep calm, but ever since I had escaped, my mind could not stop racing. It just wouldn't slow down, and I felt that everyone was out to get me.

Finally, the mzungu told me that a man and woman were there to see me. However, when they came in, it was not my father and mother but my stepmother and my uncle. At first they did not even recognize me. It had been many years since the day I was abducted, and life had changed me too much. After looking deeply into my eyes for a minute, my stepmom recognized me. She ran to me and cried so much. I told her not to cry.

I kept saying, "I'm here, I'm here. You shouldn't cry now. I'm alive."

Heather

CHILDVOICE VOLUNTEER

AUGUST 14, 2009

"I don't know how it started, but we sang and danced, screamed and laughed; all of us were in our own world, screaming. We yelled into the rain and into the night. We screamed and sang out of joy; we screamed out of anger, sadness, happiness, and love. We screamed at the top of our lungs in release of everything. It was exciting and sad, happy and funny. I laughed so hard, but simultaneously I have never been so sad."

REJECTION AND RECOVERY

"Even if my father and mother forsake me, the Lord will take me in."

- PSALM 27:10

Grace

I don't remember a lot from the mission house, only that I had nightmares all the time that wouldn't stop. I also kept asking about my parents, but no one would give me answers. They said I needed help and I had to stay there. I didn't understand and sometimes I felt like escaping and going home myself, but I didn't. I think I stayed because for the first time in so long I had food and a bed to rest my head. Plus, I wasn't running from bullets. I also had this baby growing inside of me, about to come out. My only choice was to stay—at least it was somehow safe there.

If I tried to leave, would I even make it home?

In June I gave birth to Christopher.

My heart felt hollow. I thought about what would happen if I were still in the bush. Once you have a child there, your life can become a little easier because you get respect from people. Sometimes they will even give you more time to take care of the baby, instead of carrying heavy loads or looting. But here on the outside, a baby makes life more difficult, especially when people know that he is from the bush, a child of a rebel.

Soon after, my stepmother came for me. Why didn't my mother come? When I asked, she said that Momma was still at home waiting for me. I thought, "If Momma is there, why didn't she come to me herself?" I didn't ask this, and we traveled home together. When we got close to our home, I saw more people I knew and started asking, "Where is my mother? I need to find her. I need to see my father." No one would give me a straight answer. Right before we reached our village, my uncle came and told me the truth, the truth that I knew all along in my heart but did not want to hear—my parents were dead.

Immediately when I heard this I felt a pain in my heart that was worse than I had ever felt in the bush. My parents were gone and I was alone; what could I do? What did I have to live for now? My world had stopped, but my mind was racing. I started to think maybe it would be better for me to go back with the rebels. I could forget about all I had lost at home.

My sadness quickly turned into anger over what had become of my life and my family. Part of me also wanted to go back to the bush and kill other people's mothers because that is what we did in the bush. If someone wronged us, they would be punished. But who was there to blame for this?

No, I wanted to go back to the bush to die.

That was all I could do.

After some time, I found out what really happened to my parents. Not long after the rebels had abducted me and we made it to Sudan, some of them came back to abduct more children from my village. They had found my parents and beat them until they were unconscious. They took many children at the same time, so there was a lot of confusion. The neighbors could not say for sure what happened to my parents after that. Some said Daddy was in a red shirt and was mistakenly killed because the rebels thought he was someone else. No one could say anything about my mom, or maybe they really knew but did not want to tell me the horrible truth.

All they could say for sure is that this was the day they had died.

Even though it had been my home at one time, I could not stay there anymore. Too many bad things had happened, and it would only cause me pain. There were some people who were happy to see me. In my family, there were only my brothers and sister, my brother's wife, my stepmom, and my uncle. When I was in the bush, they said people on the outside could not be trusted and wanted to kill us. They were right about some people. Even some of my own extended family were not happy to see me. They said I should die because I was a rebel and would always be a rebel.

I had never known this kind of rejection before.

143

I started to become very worried about my future.

What was I going to do now? How would I take care of myself? I went back to the counselor at the mission house and told her that I wanted to go back to school. They sent me to a primary school in town. I must have been nineteen at the time, but I had to enter at the fourth grade level. I was having problems in my head and could not concentrate on my work. The environment was so strange to me; I argued and caused problems with the teachers and other students. I dropped out of school that same year. I needed to rest my head.

I left my family and decided to stay in town on my own.

I needed to find a way to learn a skill so I could make money for Christopher and me. I started going to a tailoring school where I did a six-month sewing course. While I was in tailoring school, I found a husband, but my father-in-law and mother-in-law did not want me as part of the family because I had been in the bush. I struggled through and received a certificate for my tailoring program.

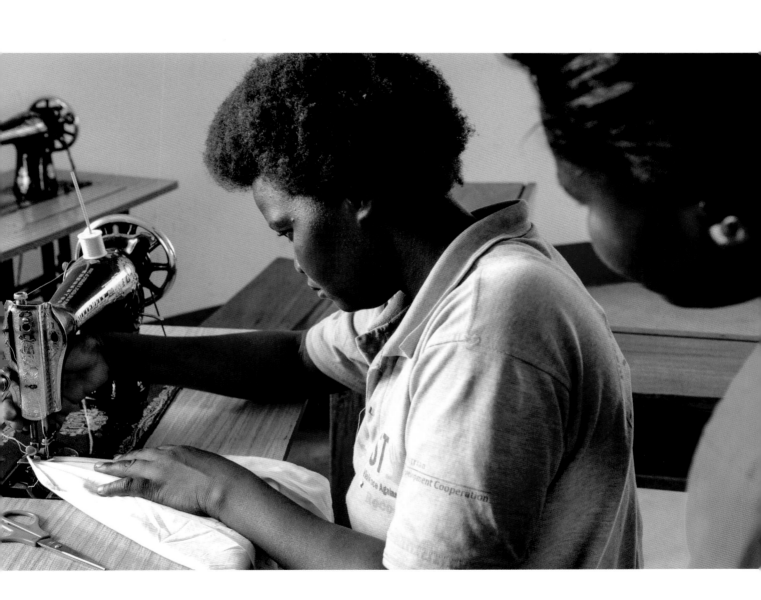

I tried to stay with my husband and had my daughter, Gladys, with him, but life was so unstable. He had other wives, and I could not get along with them. They would talk about me behind my back, accusing me of stealing and killing. I had to leave because if I were to continue that life, I might have really killed them. I was so angry all the time. Maybe what they said about me was right.

Maybe I would always be a rebel.

Richard

CHILDVOICE STAFF

Richard is the Head of Office for ChildVoice in Uganda. He has played a key role in the organization's development since before it was established in 2006.

My family and I lived safely in Kampala, but my heart insisted that I go to Gulu. Others in the south would not go to the north. They wanted nothing to do with it, but I was not afraid because I have lived through much war in my life. People would ask, "Why do you go there? What do you have to gain?" But sincerely, when you saw people in the camp, you could just cry. I would look at people and want to cry because they were living like animals. They were miserable, dying of hunger—just unbelievable. The girls slept in huts with no doors, only to be raped at night. I thought, "No. People should not live this way; this is not the way it is supposed to be." I just felt I needed to work here, and I felt it was God telling me that.

The first thing we did at ChildVoice was to make doors and bring them to people in the camps for protection. You would find 10 people or more in one hut, just trying to find safety. We were able to give 35 doors, but we knew it was not enough. It has been the blessing of my life to have seen those girls before and know that they have changed completely for the better.

They had no love at all, but now they can love and be loved.

FINDING THE LIGHT

"But now, thus says the Lord, who created you, Jacob, and formed you, Israel: Do not fear, for I have redeemed you; I have called you by name: you are mine. When you pass through waters, I will be with you; through rivers, you shall not be swept away. When you walk through fire, you shall not be burned, nor will flames consume you."

ISAIAH 43:1-2

Grace

When the rebels took me, I was living in the IDP camps. Then I came back home and again I was living in the camps. They told us we had to live there because it was too dangerous on the outside, but sometimes it seemed more dangerous on the inside. People were packed in, and there was not enough of anything—space, shelter, food, water. There was so much fighting and violence in these places, and the rebels were not even there. Many of us girls had to sleep together for protection from the men, since we had no father or husband to protect us.

I never felt safe.

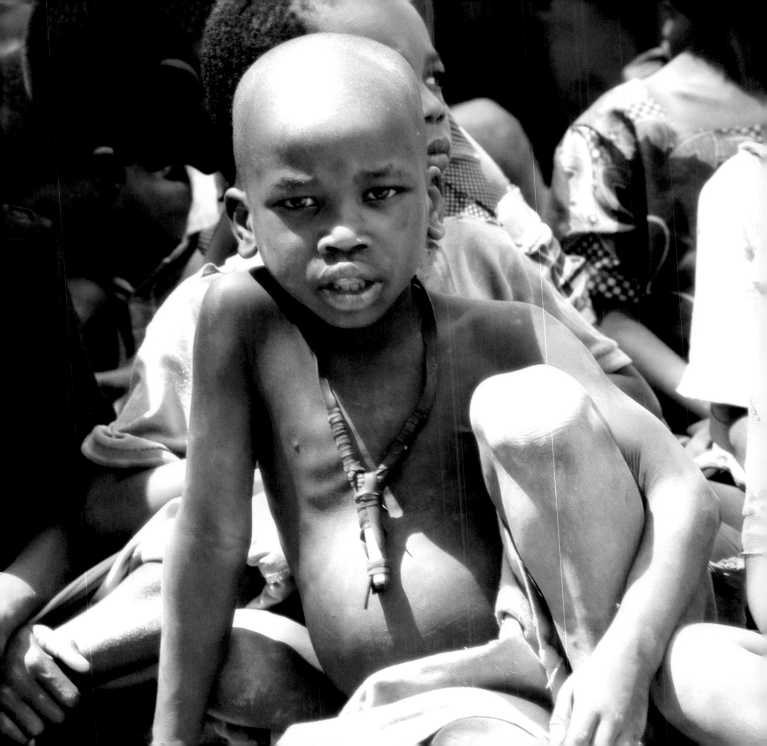

There was also not enough work for me to distract my mind.

I was constantly surrounded by people, but I was lonely and struggling to live peacefully with them. I would sit for hours at a time thinking about my life and what it would be like if I had never been abducted. Maybe I would still have a family and my friends and those around me would not treat me as if I were someone to be hated and feared. I would have a more peaceful mind, instead of so much anger and memories from my past that tormented me day and night.

It was a problem even for my son.

The people around us treated him differently because of me. Growing up in the village, I learned that we were all one family; we took care of our neighbors and their children. That was how we survived. That was not the case in the camps. Instead, my Christopher was treated as an outcast, even though he had done nothing. They would insult and abuse him, calling him a "demon of the bush" all because he was my child, the son of a rebel.

If there is something beyond hopelessness, I was there. I did not know what to do. I was trying so many things to be okay, but everywhere I turned I was defeated.

Then I met some mzungus and Ugandans who came to our camp to talk to the child mothers like me. They spoke of a place that could help us called ChildVoice. They said they would teach us things that would help us and our children to live better lives. I didn't really believe them. I didn't see why they would be different from anyone else. In my mind, there was no real hope for my future to change. But when they asked me to go there, I still said yes because at least it would be safer.

So I went.

When I reached the ChildVoice center, my mind was in a very bad place.

We had to work together, talk and share, go to class, and many other things. I wanted to learn and do well, but the distractions in my mind kept stopping me. I could not focus and I was always angry and fighting with someone. Soon I became known as the most difficult girl at ChildVoice. Everyone feared me because I was acting aggressive and rude, especially to children. They thought that maybe I would hurt or kill them, and the truth was that I wanted to sometimes. I don't know why, but sometimes that's what my head was telling me to do.

I was also having a difficult time loving my own children. I would think about their fathers and our life in the bush. I wanted their lives to be better than mine but felt helpless to change anything. I would sit and think about my mother and how she wasn't there to teach me how to be a mother.

All of these thoughts hurt my heart and made me want to burst with anger and sadness.

But the counselors and staff were very patient with me. At first I refused to talk about things, especially my life in the bush, because it would only make the nightmares come more. I was very distrustful too. Why were they asking me all these questions?

Why did they care?

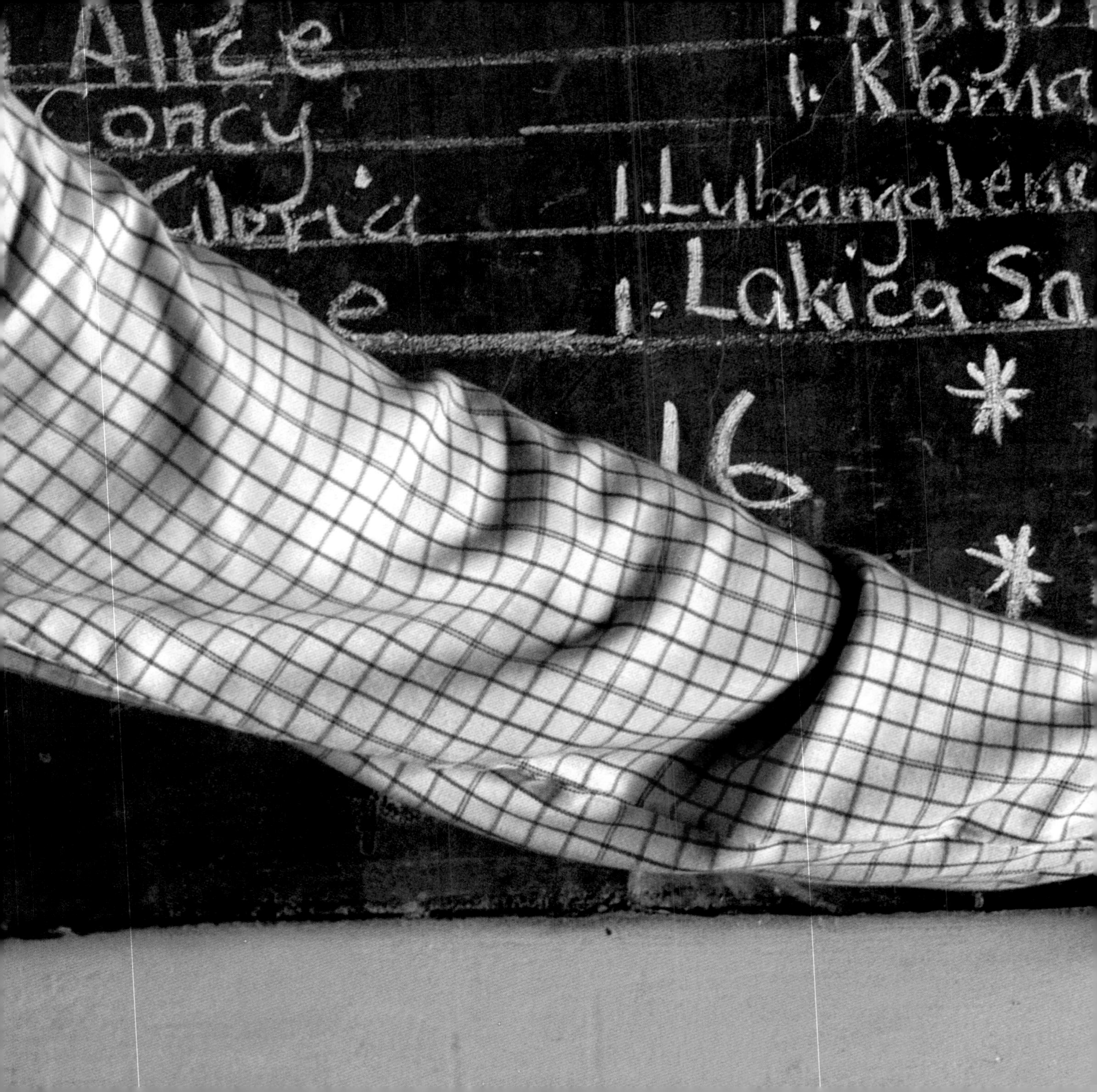
Concy
16

Moses
2. Okot Ronny.
dva

MOTHERS 30
CHILDREN 36
66

It was hard like this for some time, but slowly things began to change. Over time I saw that the people at ChildVoice really wanted to help me and I could trust them. Eventually, I could share my feelings and that's when I finally started to learn. I could say how I was really feeling and I could put words to it. Slowly these situations that once haunted me started to be calm in me again. I remember the first night that I was able to sleep through the night.

I had not truly slept for many years until then.

Nathan

CHILDVOICE VOLUNTEER

JOURNAL ENTRY: MAY 16, 2011

I am amazed. Amazed at the glory of the Lord. Amazed at the grace of His character. Amazed at His faithfulness.

Last night, I sat around a circle of people in a small hotel in the northern part of a tiny country in Africa. Something happened that is indescribable—life, hope, burdens, joy, pain, beauty in the darkness. I looked around at the faces of this strange, beautiful group of individuals and saw the glory of heaven in all its fullness. The words often fell over themselves as each shared of the day's events that challenged, excited, angered, frustrated, and filled the hearts of these people. We were a doctor, a driver, a leader, a psychologist, a pastor, a builder, a searcher, a "mamma," and an uncle—together, united.

I saw heaven in so many ways.

How is it that I have had the privilege to be a part of something like this?

What have I done to deserve this? Nothing. This is grace in my life that cannot be described in human words. Four different churches working hand-in-hand in a way that brings hope and relationship. Working as one to bring hope in a dark place. Is this what Paul was dreaming about when he wrote about the Body of Christ being one? Is this what John referred to in a letter of love for others? Is this what Jesus was indicating as He prayed for us to be united? I cannot think of anything more revelatory of those thoughts, dreams, and prayers than what I saw last night.

The burden I feel is so confusing. What can be done here? Yesterday I saw a culture that has grown completely dependent on war. I met Patrick in the street and could only think, "What will this man be in 20 years? What hope does he have for a life outside of war?" It was a thought that I have wrestled with before but never in this way. How can we really help as this community begins to rebuild? What impact will our efforts show forth? I feel selfish. I feel lost. I feel overwhelmed. I rest in the arms of an almighty God, but I wonder...

GOD IS GREAT

"'So I tell you, her many sins have been forgiven; hence, she has shown great love. But the one to whom little is forgiven, loves little.' He said to her 'Your sins are forgiven.'"

LUKE 7:47-48

Grace

Many who lived with the rebels know the place in South Sudan we call, "God is great." When I first escaped, I would see other returnees that I knew from there – people who also thought that they would never leave. Each time I saw them I would run to them and we would talk about our problems, how life used to be and how it is now. Sometimes we would remember that place, "God is great," because it was a reminder that we had been saved.

We gave it that name because of what happened there one day.

We were caught in a bad fight and it seemed there was no way out. Our attackers had us trapped, and we thought for sure we would die there. But at the last moment God revealed to us a place where we could hide behind the big rock, and somehow all of our lives were spared. God protected us – just as He is doing today. So now when life is too hard, I stop and remember, "God is great" and I recall the gift He gave us. I think there must be a reason why He saved me, but for a long time I did not know what that was.

It is true that when I came from the bush I had many problems, and I know now that most of them were in my heart. Today sometimes people ask me, "How could you believe in God when there is so much evil? Think of the evil that has been done to you." I can only say, "How do you think I survived? There is One who kept me safe and led me out." Yes, I used to question if God loved me or if He even existed, but it is man who causes his own suffering, not God.

He is love and wants to protect us. I know that now.

When I was in the bush, I prayed for God to take me home and He did.

Now I pray that He continues to change my heart so that I might still love people, despite the evil in the world. I pray that He will always do miracles in my life throughout every pain and every struggle.

When my children ask me about life in the bush, I tell them the truth, because it is a part of my past and a part of who I am. There are times when we are having problems at home, and I can relate our problems to that life in the bush. Then together we figure out how to fix them. We talk about how life was and how it is today and mostly how to be grateful for what we have now.

The first time I told Christopher that he was born in the bush and his father had died, he kept quiet for a long time. He couldn't say anything. It is still hard for him now and probably always will be. He thinks that if his real father were here, maybe we would not have so many problems. As he is getting older, he is asking me more about life in the bush and about the father he will never know. Maybe he does this because he doesn't believe me or maybe because he doesn't want to believe it is true.

This is one of the hardest things, because I know the pain that he is feeling – the pain of not having your father.

Forgiveness did not come easy to me at first, and it is not easy even today. I would feel in my heart that I would rather kill that person, or maybe that he would want to kill me. For us, forgiveness did not exist in the bush, only punishment. But when I was in ChildVoice, God showed me forgiveness, and I learned how to release someone from my heart. When someone has done wrong to you, it is best to let that person go, and then you can remain happy with a clean heart.

Holding on to anger only hurts you longer.

I forgive also because others forgave me.

There are things that I did unknowingly, other things I was forced to do, or even things that I may have done with an evil heart, but we all need to learn how to forgive and be forgiven. I think about the ones who abducted me, beat me, and nearly killed me – the same ones who took away my family and ruined my home. It is not easy to forgive such people. One of the men who beat me very badly in the bush became my neighbor after we escaped. It was very hard to see him every day; it made me angry every time and I couldn't let it go. But then I saw others forgiving me for the wrongs that I had done to them, and they still chose to love me. How could I not forgive this man?

Yes, I am a changed person now and there is real happiness in my heart.

When I look at myself today, I see that God has done something great in my life. I am less angry. I love my family and friends, and they love me. I have even found joy in helping people in my community who have had difficult times. They come to me with their problems and their pain. Some of these things I can understand, so we talk together. I give them advice from what I learned, and I see happiness come into their lives, too. Some have given me the nickname, "Counselor." Before, I could never have imagined this. Now when I see people doing wrong, I am no longer silenced in fear as I once was. I speak out about it. When I see other mothers who are in distress, we talk about our problems together and we find a way forward.

I am a changed woman, but even a changed woman does not heal at once. I must carry this with me always, growing for a while, then struggling, and then growing again. I am not perfect. My journey is never-ending, but now I can move forward in strength and with confidence,

ready to endure the night.

Conrad

CHILDVOICE FOUNDER AND CEO

We had been through a lot and had come a long way with that first group of girls. At times, things were so difficult that I wondered if we were even doing any good at all. On the last night before Grace's class went home, I remember sitting outside with them on the steps, wanting to be at eye level. I asked, "What has this meant to you?" because I knew I would not get the chance to speak to them in this setting again. We had worked so hard to get them to this point, and it was very emotional for all of us.

Grace jumped to her feet to speak, except she didn't talk about ChildVoice at all. Instead, she talked about meeting Christ and learning to forgive. One by one, the girls stood up and shared similar feelings. At the end of our time, not one of them said anything about ChildVoice.

It was all about what God had done, and I couldn't have been happier.

EPILOGUE

Many years have passed since I escaped life as a child soldier. Though I will carry part of that life with me always, it no longer defines me.

I am a proud Ugandan woman, wife, mother, friend, entrepreneur, counselor, survivor, and child of God.

Once I completed the program at ChildVoice, I finally had the confidence to pursue my dreams of running a business and supporting my family. I believe I've always had a driving force behind me to work hard and accomplish something, but for many years that force was driven by anger and hate. I now live a life that revolves around love – love for my husband, children, family, and community.

Dreams for my family and children began to take shape. I met and fell in love with a man who also had many scars from being a former child soldier. I think once you have lived that life, finding a partner who understands that part of you is very important. We have our struggles, but we can be each other's best counselors, consolers, and confidants.

I should not be surprised that even though I desired to try many different businesses and use the skills I'd gathered, I was drawn back to the traditions of my people and passions of my youth. There are few things I enjoy more than working in the fields, cultivating land, and watching things grow. We have been blessed with rich, fertile land in northern Uganda. I am a farmer once again and probably will be until the Lord takes me home. Now I am the one singing in the fields with my own children, teaching them how to plant cassava, weed the millet fields, and harvest the maize crops. Passing along knowledge and traditions to my children has been a more beautiful experience than I ever imagined.

Like the fulfillment that I get from watching my garden grow, I feel such joy to see my children mature and my marriage blossom. I think about my life—where I have come from, where I have been, and what my life is now, and I can't help but cry out in thanks to a merciful God.

I used to ask God, "Why did you keep me here if only to continue suffering? What do you want from me?" Instead of sitting dormant, lamenting my time of suffering and loss, I want to take what has happened to me and use it for good. Maybe it is simply being a good mother to my children, or maybe it is sharing my story like this. I trust that my God will use me and my experience to do good somewhere, somehow. Maybe I will never know about it, but that's okay. I am at peace.

Grace

CONTRIBUTOR BIOGRAPHIES

KRISTIN BARLOW
Writer/Editor

Kristin Barlow is a project manager with ChildVoice based in Newmarket, New Hampshire, where she has worked in various areas of program development. She received her Bachelor of Science in Nutrition & Dietetics from Olivet Nazarene University and worked in Uganda with ChildVoice for four years. There she specialized in the areas of health and nutrition education and established income-generating projects within the local community. While working alongside her colleagues and community in Uganda, her passion for social justice and humanitarian development grew as she saw the transformation of lives firsthand.

NEIL MANDSAGER
Photographer

Neil Mandsager was born in Cameroon, Africa, to missionary parents. He has spent much of his childhood and adult life in Iowa. He married his wife, Kathryn, while at Wartburg College, and they have five children and six grandchildren. He said, "It was while taking photos of my kids that I began taking an interest in photography, and it has remained a hobby of mine ever since. Working with ChildVoice has given me the opportunity to return to Africa with my heart and my camera. I am humbled to have a few of my photos chosen for this book, featuring some of the most courageous and inspiring individuals I have ever met."

www.drneilphotography.com

NATALIE COMMITTEE-FATH
Writer/Editor

Natalie Committee-Fath is a public relations manager in Washington, D.C. Previously, Natalie created a microenterprise development course and loan program for young women at ChildVoice in Uganda and coordinated economic development projects with partners in the U.S., Uganda, and Malawi through an organization called E4P. Natalie received her Bachelor of Science in Journalism and Master of Business Administration from West Virginia University.

APRIL YOHE
Photographer

April Yohe is an editorial, lifestyle, fashion, and portrait photographer. She graduated with her Bachelor of Photography degree from the University of Central Florida and has been behind the lens ever since. She loves working with people in a creative environment, making her photos beautiful and fun. April visited Uganda in 2009 and captured many of the images featured in Enduring the Night.

www.aprilyohe.com

RICK AMUNDSON
Videographer

Rick Amundson said that storytelling has always been a big part of his life whether acting, dancing, or directing films and commercials. He said, "When God first called me to travel to northern Uganda, I had no idea how these war-affected women and children would change my life. Witnessing their transformations, aided by the staff and volunteers of ChildVoice, has been truly miraculous. I am honored and excited to be part of telling these stories and pray they will have a ripple effect on others who need to experience the transformative love of Jesus Christ." Rick currently lives in Iowa with his wife and two children, where he co-owns Gate House Pictures, providing video production/post production and still photography services.

www.gatehousepictures.com

MARCUS BLEASDALE
Photographer

Marcus Bleasdale is a documentary photographer who uses his work to influence policymakers around the world. His work on human rights and conflict has been shown at the U.S. Senate, the U.S. House of Representatives, The United Nations, and Houses of Parliament in the UK. Marcus' work appears in numerous publications such as The New York Times, TIME Magazine and National Geographic Magazine, and he has received numerous awards including The UNICEF Photographer of the Year Award (2004) and The Robert Capa Gold Medal (2015).

www.marcusbleasdale.com

LARRY LINDELL
Photographer

Larry Lindell has been photographing landscapes since high school, but that changed when he made a trip to Uganda. He said, "Smiling faces and loving interactions caught my attention. How could these war-torn girls who suffered unimaginable abuse have such joy and love for each other? They had been transformed from bitterness and anger to hearts of forgiveness and love. My soul had been touched deeply. I keep going back to capture these expressions to show the world the healing that ChildVoice can bring." Larry lives in West Des Moines with his wife, Gayle, and youngest daughter, Meghan. He has five children and five grandchildren.

www.larrylindellphotography.com

ACKNOWLEDGMENTS

First and foremost, we want to thank our master planner, God, who worked through others to plant the seeds of this book far before it was even a thought in our heads or hearts. We are sure that the project would not have been completed without Him as a source of strength and divine inspiration throughout these past few years.

We are also inspired by the courage and perseverance of the young women of northern Uganda such as Grace who are beacons of hope in their families and communities. Your decisions to share such deeply personal stories with us and others, though difficult, are a testament to your strength and desire to affect change in your community and in the world. Thank you for making special trips, taking time out of your days, and working with us to help make this project better. You have honored us by sharing your stories, and we hope to honor you through this work.

To all our storytellers, Beatrice Oyella, Cecila Layado, Prossy Ayaa, Sabina Atim, Heather Ballestero, Richard Kyitarinyeba, Nathan Mandsager, Conrad Mandsager and Grace Akello—we thank you for opening up a bit of your world to us, for sharing your experiences, your words, and your hearts.

We thank the wonderful staff and volunteers at ChildVoice who have supported this project and helped make it possible. You guided our efforts and acted as translators, editors, and teachers. Even more, you have selflessly dedicated your lives to loving and serving those most in need. Truly, through your hard work and sacrifice, you are paving a way for a brighter future for so many.

To early collaborators: Abby McNamara, fellow dreamer, creator and friend, who helped jumpstart this project—your inspiration was invaluable. Felix Chivandire, for being a true vehicle of spiritual encouragement. Rick Amundson and Mike Amundson who shared their incredible videography and storytelling skills to help us to get the word out about this project. Neil Mandsager, Marcus Bleasdale, Larry Lindell, and April Yoho whose powerful photography gave meaning to some of the more difficult-to-convey parts of this book and helped us to bring these stories to life. Jocelyn O'Quinn who often provided a much-needed fresh perspective through her research, writing, and editing. The team at Scorzi, for your expertise and support in digital marketing web development.

Conrad Mandsager—without your vision, determination, and faith, ChildVoice would not exist. Like so many others, we are grateful for your work to improve the lives of so many young women in northern Uganda and beyond. You have been a great advocate and mentor—thank you.

Many thanks to Jim Galvin and his team at Tenth Power Publishing, especially Lindsay Galvin and Mary Ann Lackland who patiently walked us through the publishing, editing, and design process. Your enthusiasm, encouragement, and cooperation were exactly what we needed to bring this from concept to reality.

We give special thanks to all those who believed in us and helped us to help others, especially Kathleen Brooks and others like her, whose generosity altered our lives' paths and continues the ripple of change. Thank you to those who believed in this project, sacrificed to provide financial support for it, and continue to selflessly support the work of ChildVoice, especially Roger and Jenn Proulx, Scott and Kimberly Stober, Ben and Laura Barlow, Don Simmons, and Jim Galvin.

And finally, to our amazing friends and families who patiently listened to our crazy ideas, prayed for us, and supported us along this journey. We love you and sincerely thank you.

WAYS TO TAKE ACTION

Our goal in writing this book was to put a face to some of the issues of oppression facing women worldwide and to gather support for overcoming those challenges. We hope the stories of the young women of northern Uganda inspired and enlightened you, but that is just the beginning. There are many ways you can take action in your own community.

Here are a few ideas:

- **Learn** more about the issues presented in this book. Visit **enduringthenight.com** or **childvoiceintl.org** and start educating yourself now.

- **Mobilize** your church, school, workplace, or organization to become a partner with ChildVoice in raising awareness or fundraising.

- **Host an event** to support survivors through a Bead Party featuring handmade jewelry and accessories by women from ChildVoice and the surrounding Lukome community.

- **Go** and **volunteer** with ChildVoice to apply your knowledge and practice your skills where they are needed most. Internships or group volunteer trips with ChildVoice are incredible opportunities to serve and learn from war-affected communities.

- **Start a book club** to discuss the issues of children in conflict and human trafficking presented in *Enduring the Night* as part of a social justice team, church group, or group of friends.

- **Raise your voice** if you or someone you know has experienced abuse, exploitation, or oppression. The first step in addressing these challenges is to make them known.

- **Connect** with the storytellers through **enduringthenight. com** and join the conversation at Facebook.com/childvoice and Twitter.com/ChildVoiceInternational.

We invite you to take the next steps and get involved!

STUDENTS AT THE CHILDVOICE LUKOME CENTER, UGANDA